So You Want to Save the World:

A Guide to Pursuing a Career in International Development

Jessica Ernst

Acknowledgements

I want to express my most heartfelt appreciation to Natalie Alm, Anna DeVries, Debjeet Sen, Jessica Arnett, Judy Yang, Thuy Dinh, Josephine Luu, David Saeger, Ben Foley, Bonnie Ernst, and other family and friends for their valuable feedback, thoughtful contributions, and ongoing support.

Contents

Why did I write this book?

Having been asked to advise a number of people on how to pursue a career in international development over the years, I decided to capture the conversations and hone the guidance into this book. Since most of the people I have advised have been students or recent graduates of both undergraduate and graduate programs, this book will focus on opportunities and career steps which are best applied toward the beginning of your career.

Additionally, what you will find in the following pages are questions—not mandates on what you should do, but the means to think through what you really want in an international development career. I have often found that people considering a career move have strong ideas about what they want and simply need guidance on what questions to ask themselves.

For instance, would you want to live most of your life abroad? I would venture that you had a strong response to that question. Neither yes nor no is right, as you do not have to live abroad to work in international development; but I have found your preference does open or constrict opportunities for different types of jobs. Furthermore, if you are not sure exactly what your answer is to a question asked in this book, you can still use your general thoughts on the question as a tool to move away from what you do not want.

Perhaps you are not sure if you would like to live abroad, but you are certain you would not want to be in conflict-affected or fragile countries, such as Afghanistan. Even articulating these boundaries would help to narrow the types of work you would pursue in the future away from humanitarian aid and conflict resolution, as examples.

To illustrate career paths besides my own, I have also included the experiences of other development professionals highlighted in boxes throughout the book. They were asked to describe aspects of their own careers—from volunteering in the Peace Corps to living in Kenya—why they made the decisions they did, what they enjoyed, and what they found challenging. I hope these additional perspectives are helpful in informing which choices are right for you.

By the end of this book, I hope you are able to start formulating answers to the questions I will raise to begin crafting the type of career in international development you want for yourself. You are always allowed to change your mind, but clarifying your career vision gives you, your job search, and contacts with whom you will be networking a direction in which to start.

What is my story?

When I began considering what field I would go into, I would often ask people I met how they had come to be in their field, always imagining a straight, narrow path, starting at a clear decision point to enter a profession and ending at the zenith position within that same area. As time tells us all, life is never that simple. That is why I wanted to begin by sharing my story, so far, for three reasons. First, I hope that it will give you some context for the lessons I will share in the following chapters. Second, as I will illustrate in my own career path, thinking through your personal history up to this point will offer you some general themes to use as guideposts. Lastly, I have roughly tried to label my chronological story by the questions it answers; though, it is of course not a perfect fit.

Why do you want to work in international development?

What do you want to be when you go up? It is a question we are all familiar with from our childhoods and one that I always dreaded hearing, as I never had a good answer. The types of jobs I saw around me—teachers, farmers, doctors—didn't hold any appeal for me, and I didn't know what else existed out of that bubble. What I did know was that I liked watching the evening news with my Dad. It has become a lifelong interest in current, global events, which translates into a group of news apps on my phone and a lot of time on news websites. I also liked the idea of service-of giving back. My mom served on the village board, and I often volunteered through various organizations.

With a general interest in current events and service, what sort of work could I do that would pay me? My eyes started to open during AP Government class in high school, when my teacher discussed living all over the world, as her husband's job required.

I also had my first opportunity to travel outside of North America through a Spanish club trip, which took me to Spain, France, and Italy. Combined with my love of the news, that initial exposure to the world cemented my love of international affairs.

How do you get initial experience?

In college, I often focused on Africa, as I found the region's history fascinating and its future opportunities so great. I gained additional international experience studying abroad in Durban, South Africa, and interning with the Department of State in Lusaka, Zambia and an NGO near my university.

At the beginning of my senior year, a faculty advisor convinced me to apply for a Fulbright grant, which is a State Department cultural exchange program that supports both American and foreign students, teachers, and others. I initially resisted the idea, since most student Fulbright grants are research projects, and, as a political science major, I had written a paper practically every week of school. However, I learned that I could actually apply to teach English, allowing me an exceptional opportunity to gain experience in a culture, language, and economy in a completely different region. A week before I graduated, and about seven months after I had submitted my application, I was awarded a Fulbright in Thailand. I taught English in a high school in rural Thailand, while experiencing an amazing cultural exchange program.

After returning to the U.S., I took an intensive Thai language course and worked on admissions for graduate engineering programs at the University of Wisconsin-Madison, which is near my parents' house, until starting graduate school at the Maxwell School of Syracuse University. I was convinced I was going to work for the government, in some area of focus within international development, which is why I decided to earn a

Master of Public Administration (MPA) and a Master of Arts in International Relations.

What are the different types of careers?

One day during grad school, I was discussing with one of my roommates the fact that while I was interested in many aspects of international relations, I could not seem to identify exactly what I wanted to do in my career. She pointed out that it was the theme of collaboration that was running through my work. I realized she had a point and decided to pursue that thread further. To gain more experience with collaboration, I interned with a private sector association in Uganda and the private sector office of the Millennium Challenge Corporation (a U.S. government foreign aid agency), and I published a paper on the subject. It was through these experiences that I realized that it was not just collaboration, but specifically private sector engagement that really interested me.

Where do you want to be based?

With that knowledge in hand, I started applying for jobs as I graduated. I focused my search on Washington, D.C., since I would rather be based in the U.S. and it is a hub of international development jobs. I was excited and ready to take on the world, but…I struggled to find a job. Any job. For me, it was a deflating moment (or, one could argue, an ego check), in that even with two Masters degrees, experience in developing countries, and a publication to my name, I couldn't set myself apart enough to get a job. In the end, it took me about six months to find a job in international development.

What are the different types of organizations?

Through a friend who is a returned Peace Corps volunteer sharing job postings on the Washington, D.C. returned Peace Corps volunteers listserv, I was hired by a U.S. Agency for

International Development contractor to work on emergency food aid in the Horn of Africa. The position was a solid entry-level one, but the slow pace and the reactionary nature of the work (my work was responding to disasters, while other offices try to build systems to mitigate the risks of them), led me to the Initiative for Global Development. To highlight the importance of your network, which I will cover later, it was my supervisor during my internship with the Millennium Challenge Corporation who recruited me to work there almost 3 years later.

The Initiative for Global Development is a nonprofit that engages a global network of corporate leaders to reduce poverty through business growth and investment in Africa, meaning I was finally able to work (not just intern) on private sector collaboration. Over the course of two and half years, I managed relationships with agriculture and power companies, at the CEO and senior executive level, on programming that ranged from a power purchase agreement annotated handbook for power investments in Africa to large-scale grants. For instance, I managed a Rockefeller Foundation project that engaged more than 80 companies across Africa to assess how the private sector can mitigate agricultural loss. The actionable insights from this project informed the $130 million YieldWise initiative. Like in most small organizations, I was able to have a high level of responsibility on varied projects, as I was not confined within a large bureaucracy. However, the work was demanding and the turnover became unsustainable.

Feeling the desire to explore new professional challenges—and make a bit more money—I applied online and was selected as an independent consultant with the Millennium Challenge Corporation, which I decided to use as a springboard into working for myself. With the Millennium Challenge Corporation, I developed the project strategy, framework, and budget to create partnerships with leading companies to reduce malnutrition in Indonesia. I also consulted with the Global Knowledge Initiative, a small nonprofit, where I primarily focused on sourcing, cataloging, and crafting trends and ideas into salient, forward-leaning insights for The Rockefeller Foundation.

After working as an independent consultant for about a year and half, I was recommended for a full-time position by an undergraduate connection, whom I had met through networking. I was recruited by a USAID contractor as the Knowledge Management and Training Manager with USAID's Center for Transformational Partnerships, which is where I am currently working.

I am working to build staff capacity within USAID to identify and develop partnership opportunities through the creation and delivery of training courses, webinars, and knowledge management products and tools. For me, this has been key experience in better understanding the perspective and unique constraints of the government, compared to my previous work directly managing relationships with the private sector.

We are now up to present day. What began as simply a love of current events and a general desire to give back has slowly evolved to more specific themes—international development, collaboration, private sector engagement, and the regions of Sub-Saharan Africa and Southeast Asia. When I am assessing a new opportunity, I now look for these themes. However, as you have read, it has certainly not been a clear, straight path.

Mostly, given the overwhelming opportunities within international development, I have found that it is sometimes helpful to discover what I do not like (e.g., responding to disasters) and have moved in the opposite direction (e.g., setting up systems that help build resilience). You don't need know exactly what you will be in the future. Believe me when I say that everyone is still trying to figure out what they are going to be when they grow up.

Answer the question for yourself: What is your story? What influences have led to your interest in international development? What experiences have you had thus far? Have you found any common themes in areas of interest, such as a certain sector or region?

Why do you want to work in international development?

Allow me to be blunt. If you actually answer this question with, "I want to save the world," you will be disappointed. International development is a specialized sector, staffed by professionals with decades of experience and specific expertise. For this reason, determining the type of work you want to do will allow you to focus your expertise. You will be able to have a real, measurable impact in your area of focus, but, like any work, it will be limited by factors outside of your control, which can vary from budgets to security concerns.

The sector of international development is as varied as there are countries in the world. What does it mean to be "developed" or "developing"? Of course, there are short-hand definitions of high and low income status countries, but what does development success look like? To me, better connecting the different sectors (e.g., government, nonprofits, universities, businesses, etc.) through partnership is how to best ensure that people, especially those living in extreme poverty, are able to access the products, services, and opportunities they need to improve their lives. However, while we may live in an age of globalization, there are no universal solutions.

International development is a complicated web of work, where my efforts in partnerships, as an example, will need to be coordinated with others. For instance, a partnership in agriculture may help create a market for farmers, but it might require a nonprofit with agriculture expertise to train farmers. Furthermore, the work is focused on improving the lives of people who come with their own biases, norms, and social structures, meaning that the work does not only need to fit within the local context, but also consider the viewpoints of the different stakeholders.

Within this changing sector, there are a couple of main reasons for which people decide to pursue a career in international development. I will walk through those reasons and the opportunities and challenges within them.

Purpose

The reason most often cited for wanting to work in international development is the desire to work on something that you can feel good about, which gives you a sense of purpose. I have heard some attribute their interest in international development to guilt, experiences with poverty at home or abroad, or interest for a certain location as a member of a diaspora or affinity group. No matter the reason, you will certainly get that satisfaction out of the work.

What could be nobler than trying to help people have a better life? You will be able to see how your efforts helped provide emergency supplies in humanitarian situations, led to greater access to clean water, or improved democratic governance in a country. However, be warned that progress will be slow, as projects with narrow scopes usually follow five year timelines for implementation, and you will be only a small part of a greater whole, moving the needle on certain areas but not completely changing systems.

Overall, it is important to remember that international development is a professional sector in which to build a career, and not an idealized calling. You can, and will, have an impact on the world through your work. However, it is also important to recognize that you are part of the puzzle that is progress, which will never truly be finished. Instead of trying to change the world, start with understanding what you find important, both professionally and personally, and build off that.

Travel

It goes without saying that this world has become a small place through technology, which allows you to learn about, see images of, and communicate with places all around the globe. Cheaper airline tickets have also made it more feasible for more people to afford the luxury of travel. Plus, seeing the world is fun! To date, I have been to 38 countries, and, if money were no object, I would likely just spend a year visiting others. I cannot overstate how much I have learned about history, language, social studies, and so much more from direct experiences in a country. I could not have fully appreciated the importance of conservation efforts until going on a safari in South Africa; the weight of history until viewing the millennium-year-old Borobudur Temple in Indonesia; or the challenges of infrastructure until experiencing the power outages that occur multiple times a day in Uganda.

Within international development, you will be able to travel for your work, but it will depend on your position and seniority within the organizations. First, your position will have a large impact on the amount of travel you may do. A project manager, for instance, may need to regularly conduct site visits to follow up on progress. A more skills-based position, such as a communications expert, would travel infrequently to collect communications materials. I will provide details on different types of positions later in this book.

Second, your seniority will determine your amount of travel. Since travel from headquarters is usually quite costly, senior staff will often represent their organizations at events or on site visits. Therefore, you could be helping to organize a conference; but not be sent to attend, which is an example that has personally happened to me. Like other industries, you should be prepared to put in your time and then reap the rewards. If you work in a host country, however, a decision I will discuss in more detail later, then you will be based in either the capital or larger city with greater opportunities to travel to the other parts of the country where the projects are based. You may also be able to travel within the region for trainings or conferences.

Areas of Interest

You may also have a specific topic that you naturally find yourself gravitating toward. For instance, you might be interested in areas such as public health, finance, or environmental issues. While it is still possible to be a generalist in international development, it is now more common to have some sort of a niche focus, as job opportunities seem to concentrate on specific areas. I would focus on where your interests currently are and see how they develop in the future. For instance, through taking some general requirement classes in college, my interest in environmental science was sparked. In fact, I decided to minor in it. While I now specialize in partnerships, that base of knowledge has served me well, as I worked on food aid programs with USAID, a food waste and spoilage project with the Rockefeller Foundation, and managing relationships with CEOs of agriculture companies with IGD.

Reflect on what you currently find fascinating or where you spend your free time, as these could be future areas of focus. Volunteer for an afternoon school program? That could be a training ground for a career in international development. Have an interest in technology? You could be part of a team expanding internet connectivity, developing apps to assist refugees, or leveraging drones to deliver medicines to rural locations.

Answer the question for yourself: There are many reasons that people want to work in international development. All are valid, but you should be realistic with yourself on why you are interested in the field. Below, write down the reasons you would like to work in international development.

How do you get initial experience?

In order to begin exploring a career in international development, it is helpful to get some initial experience and exposure to positions and subjects in the field. There are a number of ways to dip your toe into the world of international development careers, and, while most will cost you nothing, they will take some time (which is sometimes the scarcer of the two).

Volunteer

Research organizations based in your area with which you can volunteer. Most international development organizations are always looking for free help, whether it is for one event or on an ongoing basis. You do not need to be based in major metropolitan areas to find opportunities, though that will certainly expand the variety of organizations available to you. For instance, a friend of mine volunteered to help with the resettlement of Sudanese refugees in Des Moines, Iowa.

Before approaching an organization, consider four questions: 1) what subject or region is of interest to you; 2) what skills or expertise can you provide to the organization; 3) what time commitment will your schedule realistically permit; and 4) what would you like to get out of your experience (e.g., skills, knowledge, contacts, etc.)?

First, ask yourself what subject areas or regions of the world are most interesting to you and find organizations that focus their efforts on that. Save the Children, as an example, focuses on children, CARE has extensive activities in women's empowerment and humanitarian disasters, and Africare exclusively focuses on Africa.

Secondly, it is important to understand the skills or other expertise you can bring to the organization. For instance, do you speak another language or have a strong background in writing? Outlining these skills when you approach the organization will allow them to most effectively place you, which will ensure the experience is useful both to the organization and to you.

Additionally, being realistic about your availability—starting with a small amount of time and allowing it to expand, if feasible—means that you are neither overwhelmed by the commitment nor that the organization is disappointed by you having to reduce your hours.

Lastly, don't forget that an internship is also a learning experience for you; what do you hope to achieve by completing it? Do you want more exposure to education programming, skills on how to maintain a project budget, or grow your network in the field? Internships are a great means of gaining specific experience without the commitment of a full-time position.

Intern

Interning for an organization, as opposed to volunteering, is also an option, especially for current students or recent graduates. First, similar to the process described for volunteering, you should start by researching organizations that share your area of interest near your college or university during the school year, near where you are or could be based over breaks or after graduation, and remote internships, such as online internships through the Virtual Student Foreign Service with projects across the U.S. government. Remember to also outline the skills that you can bring and your realistic time commitment. Most organizations select interns through online applications, which mirror the job application process. An internship posting can be found on the organization's website and international development job sites, especially idealist.org.

Finally, whether the internship will be paid or not varies drastically from organization to organization, but it is usually specified in the internship description. However, the perception of interns in the sector, and the economy as a whole, is beginning to change, meaning more employers are electing to compensate interns. That be said, you should expect a stipend, at most, instead of an hourly wage.

As an example, during my undergraduate studies, I interned with a nonprofit 12 hours a week to increase international understanding in Iowa. The organization was a partner on the International Visitor Leadership Program, which is sponsored by the Department of State to bring emerging leaders to the United States for a professional exchange. I worked with a group of Moldovan news editors, who were exploring how to take advantage of the greater freedom of the press in the country.

Study Abroad

Another means to gain international development experience as a student is through study abroad opportunities. I studied abroad in South Africa, and it was formative in not only leading me to work on reducing extreme poverty but also my continued focus on Africa. The programs vary greatly by the school, but I would encourage you to consider two things.

First, what do you want to get out of a study abroad program? I would focus on building up either a language competency, or gaining experience in a specific region or organization. Study abroad in Chile, for instance, to build up your Spanish language, or study in Malaysia for experience in Southeast Asia.

To intern or volunteer with a specific organization, I would be very clear on your objectives and opportunities you could potentially have following graduation. If you have always wanted to work for the United Nations, then perhaps studying where a headquarters is located would allow you to make the contacts necessary for a future position. I would generally encourage folks to study in developing countries, as potential employers are going to want to know you have some experience in a developing country to prove you understand the work and will be able to manage if you are sent to the field. Some organizations, though, are based in a developed country. For instance, to continue the United Nations example, two United Nations organizations—the World Food Programme and Food and Agriculture Organization—are located in Rome, Italy. I would pursue opportunities based on a specific organization, however, only if you have a high degree of certainty in your interest in working there. Overall, locations in developed countries do offer a unique learning experience of their own, and I would encourage someone to study there over nowhere foreign at all.

Regardless of why you decide to study in a certain location, be sure to take advantage of tangential opportunities, such as those to volunteer, intern, attend events, or meet staff at local organizations. Participating in these activities in another country will certainly give you invaluable experience and a different perspective.

Second, be sure to discuss the financial implications of studying abroad with the study abroad office at your university or college. Some institutions lessen or increase scholarship funding if a student studies abroad and there are a number of scholarships that are only for such opportunities, such as funding set aside to cover the costs of flights to and from the study abroad country.

What is like studying abroad? David Saeger

What did you do? I studied abroad in Beijing during my junior year of college, and it was a tremendously valuable experience for me.

While there, I mostly took Chinese language classes and spent time getting accustomed to living in a foreign country.

Why did you do it? Because one of my majors was East Asian Languages and Cultures, I thought it would make sense to study abroad to improve my Mandarin. I was also eager to live in a foreign country, as I had only ever traveled to Europe prior to studying abroad.

What did you like? Even though I didn't love living in China, the experience was very helpful in framing what it might be like to live in a foreign country for an extended period of time. Looking back on it, I feel as if studying abroad is a great first step in determining if the expat life is a tenable one. While living there, I was still surrounded by other Americans and could retreat into the foreign bubble if things became too overwhelming. Having the chance to go to McDonald's with people who wouldn't judge me made it easier to try new things, like joining the badminton team or eating duck tongue. Even though I didn't want to live in China permanently, spending time there made it easier for me to travel later in life. It also helped me realize that I didn't want to live anywhere other than the US.

What did you find challenging? It might sound silly, but I wish I had known how different China was from the US. As I had limited experience abroad, I didn't have a good understanding of how different the culture would really be. Before spending any significant time in a place, I'd encourage a potential visitor to do some research about the place to which he or she would be traveling. Knowing more about China would have been very helpful for me to understand the reasons behind some of the things that frustrated me while I was there.

Courses

There are now hundreds of courses available, especially through Massive Open Online Courses (MOOCs), in areas relevant to international development, and many of them are free. Taking a course on an area of interest would give you a stronger skill set or better understanding of the subject and an appreciation of whether you find it enjoyable enough to pursue it in the future.

An example of such a provider is Coursera, which currently offers five online courses that were created with the World Bank on issues ranging from public-private partnerships to climate change. The courses are self-directed and free, allowing you to take them based on your own schedule.

Events

Another means of gaining exposure to work within the international development field is through attending events, both in person and online. Major think tanks and nonprofits/nongovernmental organizations (NGOs) often host events to discuss crucial topics or to highlight a project or report. These events feature prominent thought leaders in the different specialties, allowing you to hear about the most recent actions in the sector, the type of jargon used, and where the sector is going.

Again, start by researching the types of organizations you are interested in, and then see what events they are hosting or promoting. Even if there is not of event of interest at that moment, sign up for the organization's mailing list if you would generally like to stay current on their work. When you find events of interest, if possible, attend the events in person. Attending in person is an excellent way to get in front of the type of people who could hire you one day—the power of networking cannot be overemphasized. If you are not in the same geographic location, or not able to attend events that are often held during the day, then you can possibly watch the events online. Organizations often stream the events live or will post them as a recording a few days later. Additionally, if the event featured a project or a report, the relevant resources will also be posted on the website.

After College Opportunities

If you are completing a bachelor's degree, there are also opportunities to gain international experience that only become available after you finish your degree. Specifically, the Peace Corps is a U.S. government program that places you in a developing country for two years to support a local community; Fulbright grants are another government program that will allow you to either conduct a research project or teach English; and there are a number of different programs for teaching English abroad.

Furthermore, if you are not ready to go abroad yet, there are also domestic opportunities. For instance, AmeriCorps is a government program that pays you to serve at public and private organizations, such as nonprofits and government agencies, across the U.S., with past projects having included working with new immigrants or refugees.

<u>What is it like to be a Peace Corps Volunteer?</u> Josephine Luu

What did you do? As a Preventative Health Volunteer in Senegal, West Africa from 2013-2015, I had the opportunity to work with a group of local health volunteers who wanted to lead their own community health initiatives in their rural villages.

Why did you do it? I had been building a career for myself for over

---

5 years after completing my undergraduate degree, so the decision to leave a decent paying job to work more, for free, didn't happen overnight. I thought about the consequences of removing myself from the workforce and having a gap of two plus years on my resume. I thought about not fitting into the country I was assigned. I thought about becoming as disillusioned as the multiple returned volunteers I'd met over my five years of interviewing and researching "the Peace Corps experience." Ultimately, I joined the Peace Corps because the consequences didn't outweigh my love for learning new languages, meeting new people, and gaining a deeper understanding of worlds different than my own.

What did you like? The ability to make my own schedule and build my own projects. For some people, this drove them insane; because they were used to, or are hardwired by, having clear direction and guidance.

What did you find challenging? As someone on the older end of the spectrum, I was not ready for the wide range of ages, maturity, and life experiences (or lack thereof). The hardest part was coming to terms with and overcoming my unconscious biases of my peers and administrative leaders, given I had become accustomed to a corporate life that recruits much differently than the Peace Corps.

<u>What is it like to be a Fulbright grantee?</u> Anna DeVries

What did you do? Fulbright English Teaching Assistant (ETA) in Indonesia

Why did you do it? Spending a year with the Fulbright Program is great way to "be on the ground" in a different country, which sets you apart from peers whose knowledge base and perspective is formed from classroom learning and vacation. I also was able to extend my grant for a second year to continue expanding my language skills and gain exposure to a different region of the country.

What did you like? In my experience, ETAs were quite integrated with their communities as schools are one of the main pillars of the community and through teachers, students, and their parents I could gain first-hand insights into culture and society. There are few other circumstances that afford you that kind of access. These experiences and lessons learned easily translated into project management, cross-cultural communication, and superb problem solving skills that are incredibly useful for future jobs and experiences. Also, being a part of a network like the Fulbright program confers many additional benefits such as waiving post-grad application fees for many universities, access to great networks of high-level professionals, state department alumni resources, a name brand on your resume, and most recently Non-Competitive Eligibility (NCE) special hiring status that allows you to skip public competition for certain federal positions – be warned however, that while some of these benefits are lifelong, others are time sensitive and limited to the year you complete your Fulbright until only 1 year after.

What did you find challenging? After two years teaching English, I knew I didn't want to be a teacher. Teaching is difficult and it is easy for over-achievers to be discouraged by not seeing clear results from my primary responsibilities and purpose. However, most ETAs will tell you that the value of their grant was not from the classroom, but from all the other lessons, experiences, and relationships outside of that time. Learn what you can from interacting with students – being able to explain things clearly and keep people engaged is a useful skill for wherever you go! – but don't underestimate the value of seeking to understand a culture that is different than what is familiar and the relationships that tie you to that place. In many ways, it will be an opportunity to put your college degree into practice, while still in an intensive learning mindset.

Answer the question for yourself: How will you gain initial experience in international development in your own life? Below, list how you would like to start engaging in activities with an international development focus (e.g., volunteering, courses, etc.) and the first steps you will take to become involved.

What are the different types of careers?

Now that you have gained some initial exposure to international development, the next question to ask yourself is: "What type of position would I like?" Below are the different categories within which jobs are currently classified. While the sector is slowly changing to better reflect the utility of having workers who have skills and expertise that overlap multiple categories, such as not subdividing water and nutrition specialties, hiring decisions are still made within certain traditional categories. To arm you for a productive employment search, I am giving you a realistic picture of what employers are looking for today in the hope that you will help the transition to what it should be tomorrow.

Categories within international development are divided by skills, subjects, and geography.

Skills

Skill-based positions are those that usually support the project or the organizations in general and are not always directly tied to the work. Like any organization, the international development sector has positions that support the work being implemented. A communications professional, for instance, has a unique set of skills in sharing the work of the different projects, but may not have a background in international affairs. Other positions within a skills position would include human resources, finance, administrative functions, and project management. A skills-based position that is unique to international development could be business development or fundraising. This person continually searches and networks around upcoming business opportunities, reviews the solicitations from donors, develops program design, drafts proposals, and may even work on recruiting personnel.

Subject

A second category of careers are subject-based positions, which are those where the person has a particular area of expertise. For instance, subject-based expertise can be in a certain sector, such as water, sanitation, and hygiene (WASH), agriculture, or nutrition. Experts in these fields often have advanced degrees in the subjects or many years of experience, especially in developing countries. Another subject expertise that is common in international development is Monitoring and Evaluation (M&E), which is capturing the impact of projects and improving future projects based on lessons learned.

Geography

A third category of positions are those based on geography. These professionals have deep knowledge of the political, social, and cultural aspects of a country or region, including speaking at least one of the local languages. It has been my experience that most people gain this in-depth appreciation of a given geography through living there long-term, such as through Peace Corps. However, given the impact of globalization, I have found that this type of position is no longer as prominent. The expectation now is that a person will be able to apply their skills or subject of expertise within any context, and that they will be able to become familiar with that context quickly and independently.

For instance, while I had experience in the region of Southeast Asia, I had never worked in Indonesia before my contract with the Millennium Challenge Corporation. They hired me for my expertise in public-private partnerships instead and provided me with context—through explanations, suggested readings, and my engagement within the country—as we went. There will always be an ongoing compromise between being an expert in the subject your project covers and the local context within which you are working.

Why is understanding the context so important? I can provide a general example. It has long been understood that the increased use of bednets reduces deaths from malaria, so a number of different programs have given them out for free in developing countries. However, not thinking through the local context has led to a number of unintended consequences. In countries that already had bednet manufacturers, for instance, most were bankrupted by the flood of free bednets on the market; why would consumers pay for what they can get for free? The bednets were also sometimes not used for their intended purpose but, instead, as fishing nets. Engaging with the local community, and understanding the local food security situation, could have mitigated such outcomes.

That said, it is crucial to have at least some experience in a developing region to understand the general types of situations in which a project could be implemented. For instance, in the past, computer companies have donated entire computer labs to schools in developing countries, not understanding the frequent power outages experienced in many regions. Having a base level of experience in one developing country or region, while obviously not directly comparable to others, provides you with a starting point for understanding others. As people gain experience in a given country or region, I have often found that they then prefer to work on projects in those locations where they have the greatest expertise and connection.

Answer the question for yourself: What type of career (e.g., skills, subjects, and geography) appeals to you? Do you currently have experience in that type of position? What are the next steps you can take to gain or increase that experience?

What are the different types of organizations?

In addition to the type of positions, it is also crucial to evaluate different organizations. When I originally became interested in working in international development, I thought I would work for the U.S. Agency for International Development or maybe an international NGO. However, a number of other sectors also work within international development, allowing for unique opportunities.

Universities

If you are currently still in school, you can find international development work immediately and locally. Universities either operate as partners or implementers in projects or offer international programming for their students.

First, in terms of projects, universities may be asked to partner with governments, NGOs, and other organizations to conduct research. While at graduate school, as an example, I was on a capstone project team that wrote a report on updating U.S. Agency for International Development's civil society framework. Universities can also be selected for funding to implement projects. For instance, Michigan State University is known for its expertise in agriculture and often implements projects that build agricultural sectors around the world.

Second, universities offer programming that allows you to gain international exposure, as you saw in the study abroad example. University programs could also include language centers, classes that involve travel, internationally themed clubs or other social groups, and events focused on global issues.

Government

In the world of international development, I would argue that it is the national governments of developed countries, through their international development or foreign affairs agencies, that take the lead in terms of the research, program objectives, and funding. For instance, the U.S. government, through Agency Priority Goals developed by USAID and Department State, has recently focused on food security, climate change, and global health, while also funding programming in other areas.

Focusing on these areas not only results in increased engagement around potential solutions, but it also brings in other donor governments, foundations, and nonprofits, which also fund efforts that align with the general development goal. While this leads to great progress, it also means that priority areas can change based on political circumstances and that other crucial sectors are neglected.

Additionally, there are many institutions within a government that touch on international development in different ways. While the institutions I will use as examples in this section will be those of the U.S. government, as I know it best, similar institutions can be found in other governments.

First, there are federal agencies that completely focus on development objectives, such as the U.S. Agency for International Development (USAID), Millennium Challenge Corporation (MCC), and U.S. African Development Foundation. These organizations primarily provide grants or contracts to nonprofits that implement the work. For instance, if USAID wants to train teachers in a country to improve education outcomes, they would list a Request for Proposals (RFP) for a contract or a Request for Applications (RFA) for grants on government procurement websites. Implementing organizations, such as Mercy Corps, Save the Children, and FHI 360, will submit a proposal or application. The organization that is selected will receiving funding to implement the program, which will usually last from three to five years.

Another type of organization within the government is one that works to support private sector activities in emerging markets. Specifically, the Overseas Private Investment Corporation (OPIC), Import-Export Bank, Department of Commerce, U.S. Department of Trade and Development Agency (USTDA), and Department of Agriculture all support economic growth in developing countries. For instance, OPIC uses a number of financial instruments to leverage private capital for investments in developing countries. Political risk insurance, as an example, protects U.S. companies or nonprofits if their investments within an emerging market suffer from political interference (which can vary from war to certain local currency restrictions).

Additionally, some agencies within the government also work on less traditional aspects of international development. For instance, the Department of Justice has projects to build the capacity of the judiciary and police departments in foreign countries. The Department of Defense provides assistance in emergencies, such as delivering supplies and personnel, as well as training foreign militaries to combat terrorism, drug trafficking, among other missions.

<u>What is it like working for the State Department?</u> Natalie Alm

What did you do? I worked as a contractor at the State Department for almost three years (2013-2016), in several roles in the Bureau of Consular Affairs and the Secretary's Office of Global Partnerships (S/GP). My main role was to manage communications for S/GP, including designing the overall

---

communications strategy for the office and the partnerships we managed (anything from tech entrepreneurship in Africa to a hackathon for sustainable fishing); drafting blogs, press releases, and other pieces for State Department and external channels; running several social media accounts; planning events and conferences, and coordinating a public-private partnership award. I also was the site lead for the other contractors in my office, which gave me an interesting view into the more back-end world of government contracting.

Why did you do it? I kind of fell into this position, as I had been focusing my search more on the implementation side of things within international development, but it turned out to be a great opportunity to work with a huge variety of outside organizations and meet colleagues throughout the Department and the U.S. government (especially USAID). I also realized that I enjoyed telling the story of our various partnerships and trying to figure out who else we could reach out to or work with that would be interested—the "pitch" is always fun! And as getting into the federal government seems to be getting harder and harder, contracting is one of the best ways to "get in" (even if you hope to convert to a federal position).

What did you like? My particular office was fairly new in the State Department, so I loved that I had the flexibility to try new things and be innovative—not what you might expect from the State Department! I definitely took advantage of any opportunity to attend events and talks while I was there, meet colleagues from around the building, and appreciate the respect that the institution carries around the world.

What did you find challenging? State can be challenging in that there is high turnover (from foreign service officers moving onto their next position, but also among contractors, interns and fellows, and political appointees), so you're constantly having to re-learn who to talk to, how to do things, etc. State also has a very high learning curve—you have to learn dozens of acronyms, formats and processes for "clearing paper" (approving documents), and more, often with little training.

Do you have any advice? My interns and colleagues that were most successful were ones that were entrepreneurial, didn't need a lot of hand holding, and were willing to go the extra mile and find new opportunities and projects that added value to the organization (not just wait to be tasked). For instance, one intern liked graphic design and infographics, and designed new graphics and videos for the office—something that was not necessarily on my short-term list, but turned out to be quite useful!

Finally, there are government organizations that are focused on building international relationships. Specifically, the U.S. Department of State and Peace Corps have offices and programs all around the world to engage with people where they are. I previously mentioned Peace Corps as an opportunity to gain international experience through living and volunteering in a developing country for a modest stipend, but Peace Corps itself employs professionals to run the placement, training, and ongoing assistance to the volunteers in both Washington, D.C. and local country offices.

The State Department has a much wider mission, which includes monitoring the political, economic, and social issues within countries and communicating American policy and culture to the rest of the world. What does this mean in terms of actual jobs? There are foreign service officers (FSOs) who are placed in countries around the world, including capitals in the developed world, with the responsibility to perform consular services, report on political and economic developments in the country, and share U.S. culture (as an intern with the U.S. Embassy in Zambia, I supported the opening of an exhibit of Harlem Renaissance paintings in the Lusaka National Museum).

FSOs rotate every two to three years, depending on their preference and the type of post (e.g., more dangerous locations often have shorter assignment times). State Department staff based in the U.S. work on issues as varied as issuing passports, managing international programs (e.g., Fulbright and International Visitor Leadership Program), and compiling, analyzing, and reporting on international trends (e.g., Human Rights Reports, Country Reports on Terrorism, Trafficking in Persons report).

NGOs/Nonprofits

The label of non-governmental organizations (NGOs), commonly known as nonprofits in the U.S., represents a large number of organizations that vary greatly. It's important to note that while it is common to refer to NGOs as nonprofits, as I have done in this book, there are development organizations which have governance structures that do not fit within the not-for-profit legal structure.

For instance, in the U.S., the largest organizations that implement international development programs are for-profit. Primarily funded by the U.S. Agency for International Development, organizations like Chemonics and DAI are privately owned. Within the development community, there are understandably mixed reactions to for-profit firms (sometimes called "Beltway bandits") implementing development programming.

Some argue that since these organizations are only implementing programs for the money, they will cut corners to increase their profits while hurting the beneficiaries. The counterargument is that a for-profit organization is likely to be more efficient, as they want to obtain the best development result at the lowest cost. Like most binary arguments, the truth is somewhere in the middle and depends on the organization.

Beyond the for-profit or nonprofit status, NGOs also vary in missions that range from supporting efforts in one key area (e.g., assisting women suffering from fistula) to those that employ experts in all sectors. Furthermore, NGOs can range in scale from local, in-country organizations that work in a specific community to international NGOs that implement projects around the world.

One means to differentiate NGOs and nonprofits is through understanding the two distinct roles they play in international development. Specifically, organizations can be considered by the function they serve and the subject on which they focus. In terms of function, nonprofits usually act as either an implementer or advocacy organization.

Implementing organizations are those in developing countries performing the work. When you have seen video of aid workers distributing food aid, building wells, or training farmers in far flung locations around the world, it is the implementing organizations you are seeing. While government agencies, such as USAID, do also have presences in developing countries, their role has largely become one of a funder—designing, awarding, and monitoring projects. In contrast, implementers are usually non-governmental or multilateral (e.g., United Nations) organizations that receive funding from donors to carry out a project in a certain country or region. The work itself can vary from delivering humanitarian assistance to supplying expert advisors on country policies. Implementers will have people in-country directly managing the projects and also a broad headquarters staff to support the project with budget, human resources, communications, and other services.

In the U.S., implementers also provide direct staffing support to USAID through institutional support contracts, which can vary from employing administrative assistants to senior experts. My current position with USAID is through an institutional support contract.

Some of the largest implementers include FHI360, Catholic Relief Services (CRS), Jhpiego, Save the Children, International Rescue Committee (IRC), and Mercy Corps, among others. One place to start to learn more about implementers is through USAID's website, which publishes a list of its top 40 funding recipients.

What is it like to work for a NGO? Chris

What did you do? I've worked for two different NGO's. Both focus primarily on building the capacity of agricultural and agricultural related enterprises. In my current position I manage a USAID funded horticulture production and marketing project. Most of my job involves working with our field team to ensure that we're on track to meet all of the goals we set forth in our approved proposal, which includes drafting and implementing technical strategies and approaches, overseeing the operations and administration of the project, tracking and managing project finances, managing the multiple subawardees on the project, and communicating with both USAID and the host government to ensure both are happy and informed of the project's activities.

Why did you do it? I've worked both on a support contract for

---

USAID projects as well as a business analyst developing new systems and change management approaches for USAID. I found myself wanting to be more directly involved with actual development work. Since USAID and other donors tend to not be involved in direct project implementation, working at an NGO allows me to have a couple projects that I am involved in at a granular level.

What did you like? The best part of working in project management at an NGO is that you have the flexibility to specialize in a variety of topics and have a range of experiences. One day I might be rewriting personnel policy, then the next I'm drafting our technical approach for value chain development, then meeting with our finance staff to make sure we're on track to meet our spending targets. Project management also provides plenty of opportunities to travel to the field to assist project staff and monitoring activities firsthand.

What did you find challenging? One of the biggest challenges is the similar to what I mentioned previously as a perk. Since I'm not a purely technical person, I often have to become an expert, or at least fairly knowledgeable, on very different things in a short period. Project management means being able to select which health care plan is best for your project staff, knowing the best way to implement a grants program, how to write strategy documents, and how to create an effective budget tracker all at the same time. Having to go from one specialization to another means that you aren't able to develop an in-depth and long term knowledge base for one subject.

A second function that an organization can have is to be an advocate for a specific issue. For instance, Human Rights Watch monitors and advocates for the protection of human rights around the world. These organizations are often laser focused on one specific issue, continually pushing for greater awareness and funding for it. While it is possible for implementing organizations to play an advocacy role, such as encouraging a policy change for an area that they work on, it is not usually their main focus. Also, depending on their legal structure, some organizations may be limited in the amount of advocacy work they can undertake.

Additionally, nonprofits can be organized through the subject areas on which they focus. For instance, some organizations, such as CARE, Save the Children, and CRS, are known for their work in humanitarian assistance or disaster response. Other organizations have particular expertise in health, environment, agriculture, education, economic development, among others.

Private Sector

Companies engage in international development efforts that range from completely philanthropic (e.g., providing funding or free items) to activities that enhance their core business. Given that this is my area of interest, I could write an entire book just on this area, but I will try to provide just an overview. I would generally categorize international development roles for private companies into three types: philanthropy, shared value (sometimes still called corporate social responsibility [CSR]), and corporate foundations.

First, philanthropic contributions are those that have no direct benefit for the business, beyond potentially good public relations. For instance, FedEx and UPS have both leveraged their logistics networks and expertise to support the rapid delivery of supplies to disaster areas around the world. Since donating either money or supplies is not sustainable, there is a often a separate office within a company that is established to disperse philanthropic funding, and, given the dual benefits of working for the company and directly doing good, it is usually staffed by people promoted from within the company.

Next, shared value refers to development investments that support the core business of the company. The Coca-Cola Company, as an example, has invested heavily in clean water initiatives. While this has clear health and environmental benefits for local people, it is also beneficial to Coca-Cola, as it takes more than two liters of water to produce one liter of Coca-Cola. Decisions on what to fund are often made by either a core team in headquarters or individuals dispersed in different regions or countries around the world. Furthermore, some investors have begun focusing part or all of their investments in emerging markets or social businesses in order to meet the demand for more socially conscious investments or to benefit from higher returns that can be possible in developing markets.

Finally, companies often also establish corporate foundations, which are completely separate legal entities but entirely funded by the company. These foundations often work in areas that complement the business but, for legal reasons, cannot directly benefit it. For instance, the Walmart Foundation, which provides grants both domestically and internationally, partnered with USAID to train women farmers in Latin America as part of its "Global Women's Economic Empowerment Initiative." While the selected value chains are often those that Walmart sources, the farmers are encouraged to sell to whichever company offers the best price for their commodities.

Additionally, there is a new, growing category of companies called social businesses. Instead of measuring business success through the return on investment, these companies emphasize their social impact while ensuring financial sustainability—often referring to a double bottom line. Examples include solar light providers in areas currently served by kerosene lanterns, urban sanitation facilities, and recycling centers. Since this area and the companies themselves are still new, the viability and effectiveness of the model are still being determined.

Foundations

While many of the largest foundations have been working internationally for decades, the size and scope of international efforts have drastically increased with the establishment of more recent foundations, such as the Bill and Melinda Gates Foundation and the Open Society Foundation. Most foundations publicly state their main areas of work, such as The Rockefeller Foundation's focus on resilience, which allows you to determine whether the organization shares your subject or geographic area of interest. As foundations are primarily funding organizations and do not implement their own programming, positions with a foundation will often involve significant project and grant management.

International Organizations

Finally, international organizations, which include the United Nations, World Bank, and regional development banks, also focus on international development. The distinguishing feature of an international organization is that it is comprised of countries as members. The mission, stakeholders, and types of positions vary drastically across the different organizations and sub-organizations, meaning you would need to focus your efforts on an organization based on your area of interest. For instance, two organizations under the World Bank Group umbrella undertake the reduction of poverty in developing countries through different avenues. The World Bank works with developing country governments to address poverty around the world through analysis and investments. The International Finance Corporation (IFC), meanwhile, provides investment services to companies in order to build a private sector in developing countries. It has been my experience that people are best able to secure roles in international organizations through internships or recruitment programs for recent graduates (i.e., UN's Young Professionals Program).

Where to Start

Now that you understand all of the players in international development, you could be forgiven for feeling overwhelmed. With so many organizations to potentially work for, how do you start your search? Follow the money. While it may not always be pretty, funding is a crucial foundation for being able to implement programs. It is also possible to trace both up and down stream. For instance, if you read about a project that you find interesting, you may think about working with the organization that is implementing it. However, you could also trace the grant or contract back up to the original funder, perhaps a foundation that shares your area of interest. You could also follow the funding down by researching the top funders and identifying the organizations that they support. The Bill and Melinda Gates Foundation, for instance, provides a database of all of their grantees on its website.

Answer the question for yourself: Are you interested in working for certain types of organizations? List those types of organizations below and the characteristics that you find most appealing. If you have already identified specific organizations within a certain category, also write them down here.

Where do you want to be based?

One final question to consider is where in the world you would like to be based. This is not a straightforward question, as the answer can change throughout your life and will require weighing different considerations. There are two lenses through which I would consider where to be based: professional and personal issues.

Professional

Your professional goals will greatly influence whether working abroad is advantageous for your career. Generally, having some experience abroad is crucial to building a career in international development, meaning, if you have not been able to gain experience through other avenues I previously described (e.g., studying abroad, Fulbright, etc.), then taking a position abroad may allow you to gain experience in a developing country.

Since donors are now emphasizing building local capacity through hiring more local staff, most positions for expatriates abroad are for high-level staff. I would suggest reaching out directly to a local country office, not headquarters, to learn about potential positions. However, it is crucial to speak the local language and have at least some familiarity with the country (while having lived in the country would be ideal, research papers, internships in organizations focused on the country or region, or similar work during college would support your application).

A second professional consideration for working abroad is the type of work you would like to do. If you are interested in implementing a program, then you would want to apply for the few positions based in the country. While most positions are usually based in the capital of a given country, with trips out to local implementation sites, if they are not in the capital there can be positions based throughout a country in smaller cities or rural locations.

Conversely, if you enjoy seeing the bigger picture, such as evaluating policy considerations, managing relationships with donors, or running communication campaigns, then you would want to be based at headquarters. An organization's headquarters can still be based in a country that is different than the one you live in, but it is almost always in the United States or Europe. Positions in headquarters, depending on the type of work, can also travel to program countries for short-term assignments, lasting as long as a few days to months, to support the work being work being done within the country.

Finally, the amount of money you would like to make will also play a role in your location, as people based in more dangerous locations earn more money. For instance, people based in Iraq, Afghanistan, Sudan, and Syria take on greater risk and are compensated at a higher rate. To get an idea of the amount of risk in a location, the Department of State lists the percentage that would be added to a person's salary, specifically danger pay and post differential, if they work in a given location. For instance, if you were to be working in Somalia as I am writing this, you would receive an additional 70 percent above your normal salary. That is a significant amount of money, but the country also has an active terrorist group. You will need to determine the level of risk you are comfortable with versus monetary gain.

Personal

There are a number of personal reasons why you may or may not want to be based abroad. First, while I believe you should generally do what is best for you, you do need to be aware of how your location will influence your friends and family.

First, there are social considerations. Specifically, in terms of family, if you already have a significant other and/or children, they may not be able to travel with you to certain locations, especially if the location is more dangerous. Additionally, living abroad generally translates into being away from your friends and family both in terms of distance (long plane rides mean you won't be able to come back for all of the events you would like to) and time zones (it is difficult to connect with people if you are sleeping when they are awake and vise versa).

With the distance from your friends and family, most people naturally form bonds with those with whom they share a connection, especially nationality and language. It leads to insular groups of expatriates within a country. These groups are also always changing, as people transfer to other countries or return to headquarters. Overall, I have found living in a country for more than a few months to be a lonely experience if I did not go in with an established network, such as fellow Fulbright grantees in my cohort.

Second, you will want to consider your personal security. While anything can happen in any part of the world, the security situations vary drastically depending on where you are based. For instance, obviously in fragile states, there will be a high level of security, often living in a compound with other expats and armed guards. In more stable countries, but those with high levels of crime, it has been my experience that the homes are within high fences, with a guard posted at the gate. In some countries, especially in cities, I have seen security that would compare to what is found in any large city in the United States, such as a security fob to enter a building. You will need to consider what level of insecurity you would be comfortable living in, and in terms of personal security and also living conditions.

Another personal consideration on where to be based is your personal comfort. Depending on where you are, you may not have access to goods and services you normally expect. For instance, while I was in Uganda, the power would go out a few times a day. Other potential issues in a country include a lack of indoor plumbing (both water and sewage), poor roads, and security concerns. As I mentioned, however, conditions vary drastically between countries and even within a country. I have slept, as an example, in both a rural mud hut and a brand new, urban apartment complex in Senegal. Furthermore, you may not be able to purchase preferred items, such as certain foods and brands of products.

Lastly, you want to take into consideration any personal health issues. Health facilities in developing countries vary widely, with world-class facilities to those that lack modern equipment. If you have a health issue that requires ongoing care, you will want to consult with your health care professional and employer to ensure that you will be able to access the care you need either within the country or be able to be transported to another country for treatment.

<u>What is like living abroad?</u> Debjeet Sen

What did you do? I spent several years in Kisumu in western Kenya as a maternal and child health specialist. Kisumu is a delightfully laidback town located right on the Equator on the shores of Lake Victoria—the world's largest freshwater lake in the tropics.

Why did you do it? I had always wanted to leave my desk job in

Washington, DC for a position in Africa—one that would allow me to be closer to the "action" (so as to speak) and engage meaningfully with policymakers, nurses, community health workers, and mothers and their children to design and implement public health programs that were responsive to their expressed needs. I immensely enjoyed this aspect of my stay in Africa, in that it enriched me professionally and made me better understand how public health programming took place at all levels of the health system. But more so, there is something to be said about being able to immerse oneself in another culture by living and breathing it—an immense privilege that cannot be compared to the more superficial experiences one obtains through short-term country visits made from Headquarters.

What did you like? I have immensely enjoyed the many relationships I have developed at work and outside of it, gone on some incredible adventures, and developed the first hints of understanding of a fascinating culture. I have been able to transfer some of my understanding of the culture of western Kenya to a more general familiarity with eastern and southern Africa, which in turn has been reflected in the way in which I am able to work and travel without any significant discomfort in multiple countries in the region.

What did you find challenging? Of course, I did miss certain aspects of life in the United States. Particularly, I missed outdoors recreation and the ability to go easily running and hiking on well-maintained trails. There is always the temptation to let one's fitness regimen slip as a consequence and I feel that it is important (for me at least) to have a conveniently-located gym that stays open late and on weekends.

Answer the question for yourself: Where would you like to be based? If you can, feel free to write down specific countries, otherwise, list different characteristics you would want in any location you live. Do you want to be based in the U.S.? Do you want to be abroad? Are you interested in being in conflict regions or those that are stable in growing? How will your location impact your professional goals? Do you have personal considerations for which you need to account?

What is your pitch?

Congratulations! You have asked yourself all of the crucial questions to begin a career in international development. Great—now what? Now you need to craft a pitch, also known as an elevator speech. You can use your pitch to describe your answers to others, allowing them to help you begin to achieve your goals within the international development field. You may be thinking that you are not secure enough in your answers to create such a pitch; however, it is crucial for two reasons.

First, people can only help you if they understand what you need. With a general idea of what you would like to do, the final step in the process will be to meet with professionals in the field to learn more about organizations and employment opportunities through networking. Second, articulating your career plans will help you clarify your thinking.

Remember, whatever you say is not written down in a contract, meaning you can always change your mind. In fact, people expect you will, as we all do over time. As an example, I have a friend who began her career focused on WASH, but is now an expert in maternal and child health. If it makes you feel more comfortable, end your pitch with a phrase that indicates that this is your thinking at the moment, but it is evolving through your continued conversations with those in the international development field.

There are a number of different ways to organize your pitch, and I encourage you to review other resources to find which arrangement is the most compatible to your personality. Below, I outline one way to organize your pitch and a few examples of what the pitch would sound like for someone that is currently a student or working.

Remember, your pitch should take about 30 seconds, providing a base amount of information about you without feeling like a Shakespearean monologue. Also, while it will feel awkward, practice your pitch. Trust me when I say that it is much more awkward to completely flounder at introducing yourself in a professional situation.

Below is what I consider the four key components of a pitch:

1. Who you are: Clearly state your first and last name. Maybe it is a Midwest issue—which is where I am originally from—but including your last name implies a formality we try to avoid. However, when you are meeting someone professionally, you want to ensure they heard your full name at least once, allowing them to better remember you from the crowds of other Jessicas (and Saras, Michaels, etc.).

2. What work you do or are interested in doing: State your area of interest, or consider describing it. For instance, share your interest in international education, or say how or why you are interested in international education. Depending on the person I am speaking with, I will describe my work as working in public-private partnerships or how I create partnerships to increase social impact.

3. What makes you special: Describe your professional experience or an example of your work that demonstrates your unique expertise or of which you are particularly proud.

4. What is your ask/goal: What would you like the person to do? You can either define what your goal is, which will vary by the situation, or consider asking them a question. For instance, are you interested in gaining specific advice, their thoughts on an aspect of their profession, or whether they know someone involved in a specific area of work?

Here are two examples of a complete pitch—one for a student and one for a professional.

Student

My name is Jessica Ernst. I am a graduate student at Syracuse University with an interest in international public-private partnerships. I recently gained firsthand experience of challenges companies face through an internship with a private sector association in Uganda. I am interested in learning more about your work in partnerships and any suggestions you would have for someone like me just starting out.

Professional

My name is Jessica Ernst, and I create partnerships to increase the social impact of organizations in developing countries. I'm currently working with USAID to build their international capacity to partner with the private sector. I'm at this event to learn about how others are measuring impact; how has your organization approached measuring impact?

However you decide to craft your pitch, be sure to give people enough interest and information to invite a response-whether that is a response to your question or a follow up one.

Answer the question for yourself: Using either the provided structure and examples or ones found through your research, draft your initial pitch below. Remember that this is a not a static pitch, but one that you are able to continually develop as you meet with professionals in the field and better understand your career goals.

How do you connect for networking?

With a crafted pitch, the final step for jumpstarting your career in international development is to network with professionals in the sector. I realize that this can be intimidating and nerve-racking, but networking will allow you to learn about both relevant organizations and also potential jobs that have not yet, or will not, be posted publicly.

Direct Connections

To begin the process, I suggest first reaching out to individuals to whom you are directly connected. For instance, contact your volunteer supervisor or a family friend that works for an international organization. If you are not fortunate enough to know anyone working in the sector, explore if you have any indirect contacts. Do you have a family friend that is connected to someone who works at the United Nations? Other indirect connections can be established through alumni organizations, such as those through your school or programs like Fulbright and Peace Corps. In particular, LinkedIn is useful to discover if you are connected to an organization or person indirectly; more informally, Facebook will often have affinity groups. Finally, after you have exhausted these connections, search for individuals in an organization whose profile you find interesting and email them directly.

Prioritization

After creating the list, you will want to prioritize who you believe will be the most valuable to contact first. This will require a bit a detective work. Sure, you know your aunt's friend works at a nonprofit, but which one? Has there been any news about that organization, such as a recent large award or financial challenges?

Are they hiring or recruiting interns? What type of job does she have? This may seem like a lot, but some quick internet searches will easily reveal most of it. Having this information will also help you be more prepared when you meet the person in terms of asking more helpful and insightful questions.

Contacting Your Network

As you begin contacting people, be very clear on four key points. First, specify how you are connected, if applicable. Your request is more likely to receive a response if the person knows you are in some way connected to them through their professional or personal network.

Second, clarify why you are reaching out to them. This part of your email should include two aspects: the applicable portions of your pitch as well as information from researching the person. For instance, perhaps this person works in humanitarian affairs, your same area of interest, which is why you prioritized them as a contact. Do not be shy in saying that you are reaching out them specifically because you know they work in the area you are interested in and you would like to learn more about the area and seek advice from a seasoned professional.

Third, state what you would like from them. As any networking guide will tell you, never ask for a job. Instead, request an informational interview, which is a meeting with a professional in a field in order to learn from their career journey. If possible, try to meet in-person—in a location convenient for your contact—to better connect with the person, but a Skype interview is also a standard communication tool within the industry.

Lastly, I have also found it helpful to suggest a time to connect in the initial email, as people generally seem to respond with either agreeing to the time of suggesting another. My hypothesis is that this is because it lessens the amount of replies required. Their response will also help you gauge the amount of time the person has available to meet with you, as they may suggest a 30 minute slot or one hour. Whatever the availability of your contact, accept and respect whatever amount of time they are able to share with you. Once the time and location are confirmed, I usually send a calendar invitation, or, at a minimum, send an email to confirm the meeting the day before. It astonishes me how many meetings are "forgotten" in the professional world.

Overall, keep your initial contact with the person short and to the point. You may be bursting with questions, but overwhelming them through an initial email may result in no response at all. In order to give you an idea of what that outline of an email looks like in practice, I have provided an example with the name changed below. At the time I sent this email, I was still working as an independent consultant and had never met the person I was contacting.

Jane,

I hope you are well. I was given your contact information, as we share a common interest in encouraging investments by companies doing business in emerging markets.

I am an independent consultant, currently working as the Public-Private Partnership Specialist for the Millennium Challenge Corporation's nutrition project in Indonesia. Previously, I worked for the Initiative for Global Development, a nonprofit that engages a global network of corporate leaders to reduce poverty through business growth and investment in Africa. I led the agriculture and electrical power initiatives, which included the project management of a Rockefeller Foundation grant to assess how companies can mitigate loss in agriculture. The project engaged more than 80 companies in Nigeria, Ghana, and Kenya.

I would appreciate the opportunity to meet with you to learn more about your experience facilitating investments in Africa and any guidance you have as I continue to build my career. Would you be available in the next few weeks, perhaps on Thursday, March 5th at 10 am?

Best regards,

Jessica

Meeting Preparation

Before your meeting, quickly review any information you found in your research on the person. Some time may have passed since you initially contacted them, and you want to make sure you have, at a minimum, the correct name, how you are connected with them, and their current position and organization. Your questions can then be more targeted, and hopefully more beneficial for you. For instance, if you know they formerly worked at your dream organization, they cannot only tell you what it is really like to work there, but they likely also still have a number of contacts there.

In order to provide you with the most practical advice possible, below I have provided topics to focus on during the networking meeting. However, this meeting is hopefully the first step in building a professional relationship with an interesting person, and not a one-off information extraction. That means you should bring your questions to the meeting, but do not be surprised if the path or outcome of the conversation is not exactly what you imagined. It would be great if the person had an internship ready for you to apply for that day, but, if they become a long-term contact or mentor, then they will continue to keep you in mind in the future to share additional information, connections, or employment opportunities. In fact, I have forwarded job opportunities to individuals I have met with for informational interviews.

When you do meet with your contact, focus on asking questions that let you capture how the person began a career in international development and what advice they would offer. After telling the person your brief pitch, ensure that most of the time is filled with them talking, allowing you to learn as much as possible.

Specifically, there are five key pieces of information you should focus on during your meeting. One, ask the person about the types of jobs that are represented in the area. If you are interested in working on communications, ask about the staff composition in the communications office to determine what types of jobs are available.

Two, dig into the experience and skills that are needed for the types of jobs in which you are interested. Do you need to speak a foreign language to be seriously considered, for instance, or do you need a strong quantitative analysis background? One way to ask this question is to also ask what courses the person wishes they would have focused more on in school.

Three, learn about other organizations in the sector. If there is one thing I have discovered, it is that everyone knows their main competition for funding. Ask the person who the other leaders are in your area of interest. This list of organizations will give you more sources to explore for contacts and employment opportunities.

Additionally, ask if there is anyone else with whom the person would recommend you speak. If you have made a positive impression, they may introduce you to colleagues who can also help you in discovering your career path.

Lastly, consider whether there is anything you can offer them. On the surface, this might seem silly to you—what could you possibly offer a person who is already experiencing success in a field you are just trying to break into? You might be surprised. You might have been recently taking classes in their area and can share a new research paper. Or, you may be able to connect them to a great contact you have made through your networking efforts. You do not have to force it, but, if you can think of anything to offer them during the meeting, or to follow up with them after, it is part of demonstrating that you want to build a professional relationship with the person.

After the meeting, remember to send a thank you email. The person you met with gave up valuable time to speak with you, and you should respond in a way that recognizes that. Also include any additional resources you agreed to send, such as a link to an article you discussed. If, and only if, the person requests it, share with them the most recent version of your resume.

Jessica Ernst

Answer the question for yourself: To start your networking, list people you are directly or indirectly connected to who either work in international development or can connect you to someone that does. Don't be shy! As a person who has met with students regularly for the past 5 years, everyone loves being asked for advice. Below I have outlined how you can set up your list to also include how you know this person, their contact information, and how high of a priority you consider them. Prioritizing will help you focus in on those contacts who you think we be the highest value. When you begin to contact people, I recommend aiming to email or call one person per day, as to not burn yourself out.

Name	How you know them	Contact information	Priority (1 high – 5 low)

As you start to send emails or make phone calls, it is a good idea to keep track of your outreach in terms of when you reached out. Recording this information will allow you to determine if you need to follow up. Marking down when you met and the thank you was sent is another simply way of keeping track of these steps.

Name	Date contacted	Date met	Date thank you sent

Now what?

Are you feeling overwhelmed? As counterintuitive as it sounds, that means you are on the right track. We have considered the key questions for shaping your career, and each one demands a lot of introspection and clear articulation—not an easy task!

Review each "Answer the question for yourself" section throughout the book. Do you have an answer in every one? If not, take some time to at least outline some initial thoughts to the questions you did not answer. Do not be afraid to listen to your gut and try not to overthink anything you are writing. No one will ever see them if you don't want them to, so you have the freedom to write down that (seemingly) outlandish idea. Also, as I have stated previously, you can, and likely will, change your answers as part of a normal evolution in your career. However, giving yourself an initial place to start through these answers will allow you to engage with professionals in the field through productive networking.

With all of your answers down on paper, you can now widen or deepen your lens as you like. For instance, what were the easiest, or most straightforward, questions for you to answer? Consider initially using those answers as guideposts as you write your pitch and begin networking. As an example, if you answered that a skills-based position, such as working in communications, would be of interest to you, include that in your pitch and connect with those in your network who do that type of work. However, if you found that the answers painted a more detailed picture, then certainly do not be afraid to approach contacts with a more specific concept of what you would like your career to be. A career is an individual journey, meaning it flows differently for each of us.

Now that you have completed an initial brainstorm on your future international development career, it will be for nothing if you do not start the "doing" part of the process. Formulate your pitch and begin reaching out to network. Learning from the experiences of others is the simplest way to gain an appreciation for different types of careers, organizations, and other aspects of working in international development.

After you have started to meet with professionals, you should revisit your answers to the questions and consider making revisions based on any insights gleaned from those interactions. There is no shame in initially being interested in financial management, but realizing your love of numbers better translates into M&E positions.

While you should consistently revisit and revise your answers as you learn more, it is important to remember that you are speaking to individuals and not a homogeneous sector. At an absolute minimum, I would connect with at least three different people on a given answer before drawing conclusions. One person's positive experience may have been negative for another, or their reasons for making those decisions may vary from your circumstances. Understanding the experiences of multiple people will allow you to better make those comparisons and decide which course would be best for yourself personally and professionally.

Finally, if I could ask you to remember one point from this book, it would be that you are embarking on a career full of so many amazing potential avenues that no one could know where it will lead, except toward a worldwide adventure where you will be part of improving lives. You have not chosen a career with a clearly defined path, but instead, you are in a career that offers you an incalculable amount of opportunities and challenges, with the entire world to work within! So do not worry as you work through the slow process of building your career—let the kids try to answer what they want to be when they grow up—you've got a world to save (well, at least, help)!

Checklist

In the course of this book, we have covered a lot of ground together. To pull it all together in a more compact form, below is a checklist of the steps you should do as part of considering a career in international development.

1) Read this book in its entirety: I literally have friends tell me, "Jessica, this is a really good book. Don't skim it!" I'm that known as a skimmer of books. However, I kept this book short and condensed to make it feasible for you to read it and get going quickly.

2) Answer the question with as much detail as possible: It will be tempting to say, "I'm not 100 percent sure on this answer," and leave it completely blank. I get it. Writing something down can make it feel a little too real in a scary way. You need to start somewhere, though, and you wouldn't be reading this if you didn't want to do that. Write down just a few words. Draw a picture. Do whatever works for you, but don't leave it blank!

3) Craft your pitch: Review your answers to all of the questions, and pull those threads into your pitch. You are not defining the rest of your life right now; consider this a rough sketch of the start of your career path. You can still zig, zag, or jump right off it.

4) Create a list of contacts: You have people. And those people are willing to contact their people for you, meaning you are connected to a lot of people. If you can only think of a few names, just start there, and you will be referred to others.

5) Start contacting people: It is intimidating and some people will not respond, but most people want to be helpful.

6) Set up coffee dates and phone calls: If possible, try to meet folks in person in order to make a more personal connection. If that isn't possible, Skype or Google Hangouts are great alternatives that still allow you to see their faces.

7) Prepare for those meetings: Some time may have passed since you originally contacted them, so be sure to review any information you may have found on this person. At least be clear on their name, how you are connected to them, and their current position and organization.

8) Follow up with a thank you note: Keep this quick and simple. Simply thank them for their time and follow up with anything they may have requested (hopefully, your resume!).

9) After a few meetings, review your pitch:

    a.   If it still rings true, then move onward!

    b.   If not, review your answers to see which answers are changing. Revise those answers, and then incorporate the updates into your pitch.

I hope you enjoyed reading So You Want to Save the World: A Guide to Pursuing a Career in International Development.

I invite you to leave your thoughts and reactions on Amazon.

71329417R10045